Shawls & vests

LION BRAND® SHAWL IN A BALL®

Shawl in a Ball® combines a strand of slubbed cotton with a self-striping brushed acrylic, with the look and feel of silk mohair that makes even the simplest stitches shine. Perfect for these bohemian chic vests, tunics and, yes, shawls!

About Lion Brand® Yarn Company

Lion Brand® Yarn Company is a 5th generation, family-owned and operated business, and a beloved American brand since 1878. The company is devoted to inspiring and educating knitters and crocheters with yarns, patterns, how-tos, and ideas that elevate their yarn crafting experience.

LEISURE ARTS, INC.
Maumelle, Arkansas

Fringed Kimono

SIZES

■■□□ EASY +

S/M{L/1X-2X/3X}

Finished Bust: About 42½{50½-58}"/108{128.5-147.5} cm

Finished Length: About 26{27½-29}"/66{70-73.5} cm

Note: Pattern is written for smallest size with changes for larger sizes in parentheses. When only one number is given, it applies to all sizes. To follow pattern more easily, circle all numbers pertaining to your size before beginning.

SHOPPING LIST

Yarn (Medium Weight)

LION BRAND® SHAWL IN A BALL® (Art. #828)

☐ #204 Healing Teal 2{3-4} balls

Crochet Hook

LION BRAND® crochet hook

☐ Size H-8 (5 mm) **or** size needed for gauge

Additional Supply

☐ LION BRAND® large-eyed blunt needle

GAUGE

20½ sts = about 5" (12.5 cm) and
18 rows = about 7" (18 cm) over Sc/Dc Mesh pattern.

BE SURE TO CHECK YOUR GAUGE.

PATTERN STITCH
Sc/Dc Mesh Pattern

Row 1 (RS): Ch 4 (counts as dc, ch 1), turn, sk first ch-1 sp, dc in next st, *ch 1, sk next ch-1 sp, dc in next st; rep from * across.

Row 2: Ch 1, turn, sc in first st, *ch 1, sk next ch-1 sp, sc in next st; rep from * across working last sc in 3rd ch of beg ch-4.

Rep Rows 1 and 2 for Sc/Dc Mesh pattern.

NOTES

1. Body of Kimono is worked in one piece from side to side.
2. The Sleeves are worked separately, from side to side, then sewn into armholes of Kimono.
3. Fringe is added to Sleeve and lower edges.

BODY
Left Front

Ch 108{114-120}.

Set-Up Row (WS): Sc in 2nd ch from hook, *ch 1, sk next ch, sc in next ch; rep from * to last ch – you will have 54{57-60} sc and 53{56-59} ch-1 sps in this row.

Row 1 (RS): Ch 4 (counts as dc, ch 1), turn, sk first ch-1 sp, dc in next sc, (ch 1, sk next ch-1 sp, dc in next sc) 30 times, (ch 1, sk next ch-1 sp, hdc in next sc) twice, (ch 1, sk next ch-1 sp, sc in next sc) twice, ch 1, sk next ch-1 sp, sl st in next sc; leave rem sts unworked – 32 dc, 2 hdc, 2 sc, 1 sl st and 36 ch-1 sps.

Row 2: Ch 1, turn, sk first sl st and ch-1 sp, sc in next sc, *ch 1, sk next ch-1 sp, sc in next st; rep from * across working last sc in 3rd ch of beg ch-4 – 36 sc and 35 ch-1 sps.

Row 3: Ch 4 (counts as dc, ch 1), turn, sk first ch-1 sp, dc in next sc, *ch 1, sk next ch-1 sp, dc in next sc; rep from * to last ch-1 sp, ch 1, sk last ch-1 sp, hdc in last sc, ch 1, sk beg ch-1; working over unworked sts of previous row, hdc in same sc as sl st (working over the sl st), (ch 1, sk next ch-1 sp, sc in next sc) twice, ch 1, sk next ch-1 sp, sl st in next sc; leave rem sts unworked – 35 dc, 2 hdc, 2 sc, 1 sl st and 39 ch-1 sps.

Row 4: Turn, sk first sl st, sk next ch-1 sp, sc in next sc, *ch 1, sk next ch-1 sp, sc in next st; rep from * across working last sc in 3rd ch of beg ch-4 – 39 sc and 38 ch-1 sps.

Rows 5-12{14-16}: Rep Rows 3 and 4 for 4{5-6} times – 51{54, 57} sc and 50{53-56} ch-1 sps in Row 12{14-16}.

Row 13{15-17}: Ch 4 (counts as dc, ch 1), turn, sk first ch-1 sp, dc in next sc, *ch 1, sk next ch-1 sp, dc in next sc; rep from * to last ch-1 sp, ch 1, sk last ch-1 sp, dc in last sc, ch 1, sk beg ch-1; working over unworked sts of previous row, dc in same sc as sl st, (ch 1, sk next ch-1 sp, dc in next sc) twice – 54{57-60} dc and 53{56-59} ch-1 sps.

Beg with Row 2 of pattern, work in Sc/Dc Mesh pattern for 9{11-13} rows – 54{57-60} sts and 53{56-59} ch-1 sps.

Shape First Armhole

Row 1 (RS): Ch 4 (counts as dc, ch 1), turn, sk first ch-1 sp, dc in next st, (ch 1, sk next ch-1 sp, dc in next st) 35 times; leave rem sts unworked – 37 dc and 36 ch-1 sps.

Rows 2-12{14-16}: Beg with Row 2 of pattern, work in Sc/Dc Mesh pattern for 11{13-15} rows.

Remove loop from hook. Elongate the loop, or place it on a stitch marker or safety pin, so that it does not unravel. With a separate length of yarn, ch 34{40-46} for armhole chain, join with sl st in 3rd ch of beg ch-4 of last row.
Fasten off.
Return dropped loop to hook.

Back

Row 1 (RS): Ch 4 (counts as dc, ch 1), turn, sk first ch-1 sp, dc in next st, *ch 1, sk next ch-1 sp, dc in next st; rep from * across working last dc in 3rd ch of beg ch-4; working in armhole chain, **ch 1, sk next ch, dc in next ch; rep from ** to end of armhole chain – 54{57-60} dc and 53{56-59} ch-1 sps.

Beg with Row 2 of pattern, work in Sc/Dc Mesh pattern for 39{47-55} rows.

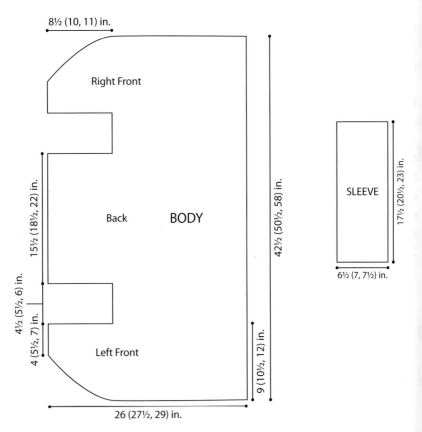

Shape Second Armhole

Rep Rows 1-12{14-16} of Shape First Armhole – 37 sts and 36 ch-1 sps.

Right Front

Row 1 (RS): Ch 37{43-49} for armhole chain, turn, dc in 6th ch from hook (5 skipped ch count as 1 base ch, first dc and ch 1), *ch 1, sk next ch, dc in next ch; rep from * to last ch of armhole chain, ch 1, sk last ch, dc in next sc, **ch 1, sk next ch-1 sp, dc in next sc; rep from ** to end of row – 54{57-60} dc and 53{56-59} ch-1 sps.

Rows 2-10{12-14}: Beg with Row 2 of pattern, work in Sc/Dc Mesh pattern for 9{11-13} rows.

Row 11{13-15}: Ch 4 (counts as dc, ch 1), turn, sk first ch-1 sp, dc in next sc, (ch 1, sk next ch-1 sp, dc in next sc) 45{48-51} times, (ch 1, sk next ch-1 sp, hdc in next sc) twice, (ch 1, sk next ch-1 sp, sc in next sc) twice, ch 1, sk next ch-1 sp, sl st in next sc; leave rem sts unworked – 47{50-53} dc, 2 hdc, 2 sc, 1 sl st, and 51{54-57} ch-1 sps.

Row 12{14-16}: Turn, sk first sl st and ch-1 sp, sc in next st, *ch 1, sk next ch-1 sp, sc in next st; rep from * across working last sc in 3rd ch of beg ch-4 – 51{54-57} sc and 50{53-56} ch-1 sps.

Row 13{15-17}: Ch 4 (counts as dc, ch 1), turn, sk first ch-1 sp, dc in next sc, *ch 1, sk next ch-1 sp, dc in next sc; rep from * to last 7 ch-1 sps, (ch 1, sk next ch-1 sp, hdc in next sc) twice, (ch 1, sk next ch-1 sp, sc in next sc) twice, ch 1, sk next ch-1 sp, sl st in next sc; leave rem sts unworked – 44{47-50} dc, 2 hdc, 2 sc, 1 sl st, and 48{51-54} ch-1 sps.

Row 14{16-18}: Turn, sk first sl st and ch-1 sp, sc in next st, *ch 1, sk next ch-1 sp, sc in next st; rep from * across working last sc in 3rd ch of beg ch-4 – 48{51-54} sc and 47{50-53} ch-1 sps.

Rep last 2 rows 4{5-6} times – 36 sc and 35 ch-1 sps in last row. Fasten off.

SLEEVES (make 2)

Note: Sleeves are worked from side to side.

Ch 28{30-32}.

Set-Up Row (WS): Sc in 2nd ch from hook, *ch 1, sk next ch, sc in next ch; rep from * across – 14{15-16} sc and 13{14-15} ch-1 sps.

Beg with Row 1 of pattern, work in Sc/Dc Mesh for 44{52-58} rows. Fasten off.

FINISHING

Fold piece and sew shoulder seams.

Lower Edge Trim

Row 1: From RS, join yarn with sc in lower left front corner; working as evenly spaced as possible along lower edge, sc in edge, *ch 1, sk about width of 1 st, sc in edge; rep from * all the way across lower edge, sc in lower right front corner.

Row 2: Ch 1, turn, sc in first sc, *ch 1, sk next sc, sc in next ch-1 sp; rep from * to last 2 sc, ch 1, sk next sc, sc in last sc.

Row 3: Ch 1, turn, sc in first sc, sc in next ch-1 sp, *ch 1, sk next sc, sc in next ch-1 sp; rep from * to last sc, sc in last sc.

Rnd 4: Ch 1, turn, sc in first sc, *ch 1, sk next sc, sc in next ch-1 sp; rep from * to last 2 sc, ch 1, sk next sc, sc in last sc; working as evenly spaced as possible along left front edge, back neck, and right front edge, **ch 1, sk about width of 1 st, sc in edge; rep from ** to beg of this rnd, ch 1; join with sl st in first sc.

Rnd 5: Ch 1, turn, sc in first ch-1 sp, *ch 1, sk next sc, sc in next ch-1 sp; rep from * to last sc, ch 1, sk last sc; join with sl st in first sc.
Fasten off.

Sleeve Trim

Row 1: From RS, join yarn with sc in corner of one Sleeve so that you are ready to work along one long edge. Rep Row 1 of lower edge trim, ending with sc in opposite corner.

Rows 2 and 3: Rep Rows 2 and 3 of lower edge trim.
Fasten off.

Rep along one long edge of 2nd Sleeve.

Sew untrimmed edge of Sleeves into armholes.

Sew underarm and Sleeve seams.

Sleeve Fringe

Cut strands of yarn about 2" (5 cm) long. For each fringe, hold 4 strands of yarn together and fold in half. Use crochet hook to draw fold through edge of Sleeve, forming a loop. Pull ends of fringe through this loop. Pull to tighten. Make 1 fringe in each ch-1 sp along Sleeve edge.
Rep for 2nd Sleeve.

Lower Back Fringe

Cut strands of yarn about 4" (10 cm) long. For each fringe, hold 4 strands of yarn together and fold in half. Use crochet hook to draw fold through lower edge of Back forming a loop. Pull ends of fringe through this loop. Pull to tighten. Make 1 fringe in each ch-1 sp along lower Back edge.

Lower Front Fringe

Make fringe same as for back along both lower front edges. Beg at side edge and work towards front corner. Cut strands for each fringe a little longer than previous fringe, beg with a 4" (10 cm) fringe at side edge and end with a 7" (18 cm) fringe at front corner.

Weave in ends.

Trim fringe evenly.

Metropolis Belted Tunic

SIZES

◼◼☐☐ EASY +

S/L{1X/3X}

Finished Bust: About 52{60}"/132{152.5} cm
Finished Length: About 29{30}"/73.5{76} cm
Note: Pattern is written for smallest size with changes for larger size in parentheses. When only one number is given, it applies to both sizes. To follow pattern more easily, circle all numbers pertaining to your size before beginning.

SHOPPING LIST

Yarn (Medium Weight)

LION BRAND® SHAWL IN A BALL® (Art. #828)

☐ #207 Feng Shui Grey - 3{4} balls

Crochet Hook

LION BRAND® crochet hook

☐ Size H-8 (5 mm) **or** size needed for gauge

Additional Supply

☐ LION BRAND® large-eyed blunt needle

GAUGE

17½ sts + 10 rows = about 4" (10 cm) over Rows 4 and 5 of Right Half.

BE SURE TO CHECK YOUR GAUGE.

NOTES

1. Tunic is made from 5 pieces: Right and Left Halves, 2 Pockets, and Belt.
2. Each Half is worked in a Dc-Eyelet pattern.
3. The Dc-Eyelet pattern consists of rows of (sc, ch 1), rows of (dc, ch 1), and rows of dc with only 4 ch-1 sps. Dc-Eyelets are tall holes formed by the ch-1 sps in dc rows.
4. Edging is worked along both long sides of each Half.
5. Halves are seamed, leaving a neck opening, to make the Tunic.
6. Pockets are worked from side to side, then sewn to Tunic.

RIGHT HALF

Ch 54{62}.

Row 1 (WS): Sc in 2nd ch from hook, *ch 1, sk next ch, sc in next ch; rep from * across – you will have 27{31} sc and 26{30} ch-1 sps in this row.

Row 2: Ch 4 (counts as dc, ch 1), turn, sk first ch-1 sp, dc in next sc, *ch 1, sk next ch-1 sp, dc in next sc; rep from * across.

Row 3: Ch 1, turn, sc in first dc, *ch 1, sk next ch-1 sp, sc in next dc; rep from * to beg ch-sp, ch 1, sc in 3rd ch of beg ch-4.

Row 4 (Dc-Eyelet Row): Ch 4 (counts as dc, ch 1), turn, sk first ch-1 sp, *(dc in next sc, dc in next ch-1 sp) 5{7} times, dc in next sc, ch 1, sk next ch-1 sp, (dc in next sc, dc in next ch-1 sp) 12 times, dc in next sc, ch 1, sk next ch-1 sp, (dc in next sc, dc in next ch-1 sp) 5{7} times, dc in next sc, ch 1, sk last ch-1 sp, dc in last sc – 49{57} dc and 4 ch-1 sps (Dc-Eyelets).

Row 5: Ch 1, turn, sc in first dc, *ch 1, sk next ch-1 sp or dc, sc in next dc; rep from * to beg ch-sp, ch 1, sc in 3rd ch of beg ch-4.

Rows 6-139{145}: Rep Rows 4 and 5 for 67{70} more times.

Next 2 Rows: Rep Rows 2 and 3. Fasten off.

Outer Edging

Row 1 (RS): From RS, join yarn with a sc in end of first row at beg of one long edge, working in ends of rows along edge, ch 1, 2 sc in end of next dc row, *ch 1, sk next sc row, 2 sc in end of next dc row; rep from * to last sc row, ch 1, sc in end of last sc row. Fasten off.

Inner Edging

Row 1 (RS): From RS, join yarn with a sc in end of last row at beg of unworked long edge of Half, working in ends of rows along edge, ch 1, 2 sc in end of next dc row, *ch 1, sk next sc row, 2 sc in end of next dc row; rep from * to last sc row, ch 1, sc in end of last sc row.

Row 2: Ch 3 (counts as dc), turn, 2 dc in first ch-1 sp, *ch 1, sk next 2 sc, 2 dc in next ch-1 sp; rep from * to last sc, dc in last sc.

Row 3: Ch 1, turn, sc in first dc, *ch 1, sk next 2 dc, 2 sc in next ch-1 sp; rep from * to last 3 sts, ch 1, sk next 2 dc, sc in top of beg ch-3.
Fasten off.

LEFT HALF

Work same as Right Half, working the inner and outer edgings on opposite sides.

POCKETS (make 2)

Note: Pockets are worked from side to side.

Ch 24.

Row 1 (WS): Sc in 2nd ch from hook, *ch 1, sk next ch, sc in next ch; rep from * across – 12 sc and 11 ch-1 sps.

Row 3: Ch 1, turn, sc in first dc, *ch 1, sk next dc, sc in next dc; rep from * to beg ch-sp, ch 1, sc in 3rd ch of beg ch – 12 sc and 11 ch-1 sps.

Rows 4-17: Rep Rows 2 and 3 seven more times.
Do NOT fasten off.

Edging

Row 1 (WS): Turn piece to work across ends of rows, 2 sc in end of next dc row, *ch 1, sk next sc row, 2 sc in end of next dc row; rep from * to last sc row, sc in last row.

Row 2: Ch 1, turn, sc in first sc, *ch 1, sk next sc, sc in next 2 sc; rep from * to last sc, sc in last sc.
Fasten off.

BELT

With 2 strands of yarn held tog, work a chain about 60{64}"/152.5{162.5} cm long.

Sc in 2nd ch from hook and in each ch across, ch 1; working along opposite side of foundation ch, sc in ch at base of each sc across, ch 1; join with sl st in first sc.
Fasten off.

Row 2 (Dc-Eyelet Row): Ch 4 (counts as dc, ch 1), turn, sk first ch-1 sp, *dc in next sc, dc in next ch-1 sp; rep from * to last sc, dc in last sc – 22 dc and 1 ch-1 sp (Dc-Eyelet).

FINISHING

From RS, lay Halves side by side with sts along inner edges matching. Beg at lower edge, sew inner edges tog for about 25{26}"/63.5{66} cm for center back seam, leave next 12" (30.5 cm) unsewn for neck, sew remaining inner edges tog for center front seam.

Fold piece along shoulders and sew side edges tog, beg at lower edge and leaving last 10{11}"/25.5{28} cm unsewn for armholes.

Sew one Pocket to each front. Arrange Pocket with column of Dc-Eyelets at top of Pocket; sew Pocket immediately above (dc, ch 1) row (Row 2) and centered between the two inner columns of Dc-Eyelets of Half.

Beg and ending at center back, thread Belt through any eyelets of Row 4.

Weave in ends.

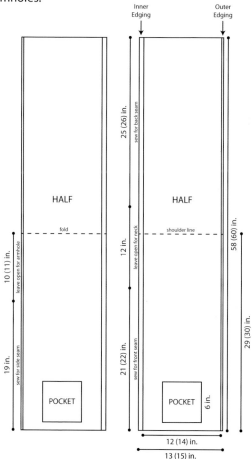

Openwork Shawl

SIZE
About 16" x 70" (40.5 cm x 178 cm)

■■□□ **EASY**

SHOPPING LIST

Yarn (Medium Weight)
LION BRAND® SHAWL IN A BALL® (Art. #828)
☐ #202 Calming Desert - 2 balls

Crochet Hook

LION BRAND® crochet hook
☐ Size G-6 (4.25 mm) **or** size needed for gauge

Additional Supply

☐ LION BRAND® large-eyed blunt needle

GAUGE
1 pattern rep = about 2¾" (7 cm).
Note: One pattern rep in Row 1 consists of one (ch 3, sc, ch 3) group and the following (dc, ch 1, dc, ch 1, dc, ch 1, dc) group. One pattern rep in other rows consists of the sts worked into one rep of previous row.

BE SURE TO CHECK YOUR GAUGE.

NOTES

1. The Shawl is worked in one piece.
2. For those who find a visual helpful, we've included a stitch diagram.

SHAWL

Ch 90.

Row 1: Dc in 6th ch from hook (5 skipped ch count as 1 base ch, first dc and ch 1), ch 1, sk next ch, dc in next ch, ch 3, sk next 3 ch, sc in next ch, ch 3, sk next 3 ch, dc in next ch, *(ch 1, sk next ch, dc in next ch) 3 times, ch 3, sk next 3 ch, sc in next ch, ch 3, sk next 3 ch, dc in next ch; rep from * to last 4 ch, (ch 1, sk next ch, dc in next ch) twice – you will have 6 (ch 3, sc, ch 3) groups, 5 (dc, ch 1, dc, ch 1, dc, ch 1, dc) groups, and a (dc, ch 1, dc, ch 1, dc) group at the beg and end of this row (for 5 pattern reps; the additional (ch 3, sc, ch 3) group and the beg and end (dc, ch 1, dc, ch 1, dc) groups combined measure a little more than one additional rep).

Row 2: Ch 3 (counts as dc), turn, (dc in next ch-1 sp, dc in next dc) twice, ch 3, sk next ch-3 sp, sc in next sc, ch 3, sk next ch-3 sp, dc in next dc, *(dc in next ch-1 sp, dc in next dc) 3 times, ch 3, sk next ch-3 sp, sc in next sc, ch 3, sk next ch-3 sp, dc in next dc; rep from * to last 2 ch-sps, dc in next ch-1 sp, dc in next dc, dc in beg ch-sp, dc in 4th ch of beg ch.

Row 3: Ch 4 (counts as dc, ch 1), turn, sk first 2 dc, dc in next dc, ch 1, sk next dc, dc in next dc, ch 3, sk next ch-3 sp, sc in next sc, ch 3, sk next

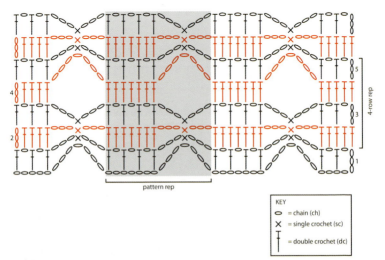

KEY	
⌒	= chain (ch)
✕	= single crochet (sc)
⊤	= double crochet (dc)

ch-3 sp, dc in next dc, *(ch 1, sk next dc, dc in next dc) 3 times, ch 3, sk next ch-3 sp, sc in next sc, ch 3, sk next ch-3 sp, dc in next dc; rep from * to last 4 dc, ch 1, sk next dc, dc in next dc, ch 1, sk next dc, dc in top of beg ch.

Row 4: Ch 3 (counts as dc), turn, (dc in next ch-1 sp, dc in next dc) twice, ch 7, sk next 2 ch-3 sps, dc in next dc, *(dc in next ch-1 sp, dc in next dc) 3 times, ch 7, sk next 2 ch-3 sps, dc in next dc; rep from * to last 2 ch-sps, dc in next ch-1 sp, dc in next dc, dc in beg ch-sp, dc in 3rd ch of beg ch.

Row 5: Ch 4 (counts as dc, ch 1), turn, sk first 2 dc, dc in next dc, ch 1, sk next dc, dc in next st, ch 3, sc in 4th ch of next ch-7 sp, ch 3, dc in next dc, *(ch 1, sk next dc, dc in next dc) 3 times, ch 3, sc in 4th ch of next ch-7 sp, ch 3, dc in next dc; rep from * to last 4 dc, ch 1, sk next dc, dc in next dc, ch 1, sk next dc, dc in top of beg ch.

Rep Rows 2–5 until piece measures about 70" (178 cm) from beg or until desired length, end with a Row 3 as the last row you work.
Fasten off.

FINISHING
Weave in ends.

Traver's Island Poncho

S/L{1X/3X}

Finished Width: About 27{33}"/68.5{84} cm, including side edging

Finished Length: About 20{22}"/51{56} cm, after folding and seaming

Note: Pattern is written for smallest size with changes for larger size in parentheses. When only one number is given, it applies to both sizes. To follow pattern more easily, circle all numbers pertaining to your size before beginning.

SHOPPING LIST

Yarn (Medium Weight) ④

LION BRAND® SHAWL IN A BALL® (Art. #828)

☐ #205 Soothing Blue - 2{3} balls

Crochet Hook

LION BRAND® crochet hook

☐ Size F-5 (3.75 mm) **or** size needed for gauge

Additional Supply

☐ LION BRAND® large-eyed blunt needle

GAUGE

2 pattern reps + 8½ rows = about 3¾" (9.5 cm) over Rows 2-7 of pattern. **Note:** In Rows 2, 3 and 7 of pattern, one pattern rep consists of a Cl and the following 5 dc. In Row 4, one pattern rep consists of a ch-3 sp and the following 5 dc. In Rows 5 and 6, one pattern rep consists of 8 dc.

BE SURE TO CHECK YOUR GAUGE.

STITCH GUIDE

CLUSTER (abbreviated Cl)

Yarn over, insert hook in indicated st and draw up a loop, yarn over and draw through 2 loops on hook (2 loops rem on hook), yarn over, insert hook in same st and draw up a loop, yarn over and draw through 2 loops on hook, yarn over and draw through all 3 loops on hook.

NOTES

1. Poncho is made from 2 identical pieces: Front and Back.
2. Front and Back are both worked from side to side with shaping for neck.
3. Sides are joined at underarms and an edging is worked around the neck.

BACK

Ch 87{95}.

First Side

Row 1 (RS): Dc in 4th ch from hook (3 skipped ch count as dc) and in next 3 ch, *ch 3, Cl in top of last dc made, sk next 3 ch, dc in next 5 ch; rep from * across – you will have 10{11} pattern reps with an additional 5 dc at beg of this row (consisting of 10{11} clusters, and 11{12} 5-dc groups).

Rows 2 and 3: Ch 3 (counts as dc), turn, dc in next 4 dc, *ch 3, Cl in top of last dc made, sk next Cl, dc in next 5 dc; rep from * across working last dc in top of beg ch.

Row 4: Ch 3 (counts as dc), turn, dc in next 4 dc, *ch 3, sk next Cl, dc in next 5 dc; rep from * across working last dc in top of beg ch-3.

Row 5: Ch 3 (counts as dc), turn, dc in next 4 dc, *3 dc in next ch-3 sp, dc in next 5 dc; rep from * across working last dc in top of beg ch-3 – 85{93} dc.

Row 6: Ch 3 (counts as dc), turn, dc in each dc across working last dc in top of beg ch-3.

Row 7: Ch 3 (counts as dc), turn, dc in next 4 dc, *ch 3, Cl in top of last dc made, sk next 3 dc, dc in next 5 dc; rep from * across working last dc in top of beg ch-3.

Rows 8-19{25}: Rep Rows 2-7 for 2{3} more times.

Shape Neck

Row 1 (WS): Turn, sl st in first 5 sts, ch 6 (counts as dc, ch 3), Cl in 3rd ch of beg ch-6, sk first Cl, dc in next 5 dc, *ch 3, Cl in top of last dc made, sk next Cl, dc in next 5 dc; rep from * across working last dc in top of beg ch-3 – 10{11} pattern reps and 1 dc at beg of this row.

Row 2: Ch 3 (counts as dc), turn, dc in next 4 dc, *ch 3, Cl in top of last dc made, sk next Cl, dc in next 5 dc; rep from * to last Cl, ch 3, Cl in top of last dc made, sk last Cl, dc in 3rd ch of beg ch-6.

Row 3: Ch 6 (counts as dc, ch 3), turn, sk first Cl, dc in next 5 dc, *ch 3, sk next Cl, dc in next 5 dc; rep from * across working last dc in top of beg ch-3.

Row 4: Ch 3 (counts as dc), turn, dc in next 4 dc, *3 dc in next ch-3 sp, dc in next 5 dc; rep from * to last beg ch-sp, 3 dc in beg ch-sp, dc in 3rd ch of beg ch-6 – 81{89} dc.

Row 5: Ch 3 (counts as dc), turn, dc in each dc across working last dc in top of beg ch-3.

Row 6: Ch 3 (counts as dc), turn, dc in next 4 dc, *ch 3, Cl in top of last dc made, sk next 3 dc, dc in next 5 dc; rep from * to last 4 dc, ch 3, Cl in top of last dc made, sk next 3 dc, dc in top of beg ch-3.

Row 7: Ch 6 (counts as dc, ch 3), turn, Cl in 3rd ch of beg ch-6, sk first Cl, *dc in next 5 dc, ch 3, Cl in top of last dc made, sk next Cl; rep from * to beg ch-3, dc in top of beg ch-3 – 10 ch-3 sps, ten 5-dc groups, and 1 dc at beg of this row.

Rows 8-13: Rep Rows 2-7 of Shape Neck.

Rows 14-18: Rep Rows 2-6 of Shape Neck.

Second Side

Row 1 (WS): Ch 6 (counts as 3 base ch and first dc), turn, dc in 4th ch from hook and in next 2 ch, dc in next dc, *ch 3, Cl in top of last dc made, sk next Cl, dc in next 5 dc; rep from * across, working last dc in top of beg ch-3 – 10{11} pattern reps with an additional 5 dc at beg of this row.

Row 2: Ch 3 (counts as dc), turn, dc in next 4 dc, *ch 3, Cl in top of last dc made, sk next Cl, dc in next 5 dc; rep from * across working last dc in top of beg ch.

Row 3: Ch 3 (counts as dc), turn, dc in next 4 dc, *ch 3, sk next Cl, dc in next 5 dc; rep from * across working last dc in top of beg ch-3.

Row 4: Ch 3 (counts as dc), turn, dc in next 4 dc, *3 dc in next ch-3 sp, dc in next 5 dc; rep from * across working last dc in top of beg ch-3 – 85{93} dc.

Row 5: Ch 3 (counts as dc), turn, dc in each dc across working last dc in top of beg ch-3.

Row 6: Ch 3 (counts as dc), turn, dc in next 4 dc, *ch 3, Cl in top of last dc made, sk next 3 dc, dc in next 5 dc; rep from * across working last dc in top of beg ch-3.

Row 7: Rep Row 2.

Rows 8-19{25}: Rep Rows 2-7 of Second Side for 2{3} times.

Row 20{26}: Rep Row 3.

Last 2 Rows (Side Edging Row): Rep Rows 4 and 5 of Second Side. Fasten off.

Side Edging

Row 1 (RS): From RS, working along opposite side of foundation ch, join yarn with sl st in ch at base of first st, ch 3 (counts as dc), dc in each ch across.

Row 2: Ch 3 (counts as dc), dc in each st across.
Fasten off.

FRONT

Make same as Back.

FINISHING

Sew shoulders.
Sew side edges together for about ½" (1.5 cm), about 10{11}"/25.5{28} cm below shoulder seam for armholes.

Neck Edging

From RS, join yarn with sc at neck edge of one shoulder seam. Work sc evenly spaced all the way around neck edge; join with sl st in first sc. Fasten off.

Weave in ends.

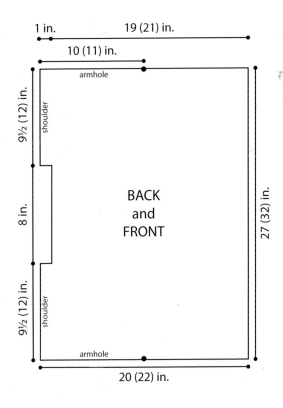

1 in. 19 (21) in.
10 (11) in.
armhole
9½ (12) in.
shoulder
8 in.
27 (32) in.
BACK
and
FRONT
9½ (12) in.
shoulder
armhole
20 (22) in.

Triangle Ruana

SIZE

Finished Length from back neck to lower point:
About 34" (86.5 cm)

Finished Width at widest: About 68" (172.5 cm)

SHOPPING LIST

Yarn (Medium Weight) 4

LION BRAND® SHAWL IN A BALL® (Art. #828)

☐ #203 Mindful Mauve - 3 balls

Crochet Hook

LION BRAND® crochet hook

☐ Size H-8 (5 mm) **or** size needed for gauge

Additional Supply

☐ LION BRAND® large-eyed blunt needle

GAUGE

1 Square = about 22½" x 22½" (57 cm x 57 cm).
15 dc + 8 rows = about 4" (10 cm).

BE SURE TO CHECK YOUR GAUGE.

STITCH GUIDE
REVERSE SINGLE CROCHET (abbreviated rev sc)
Single crochet worked from left to right (right to left, if left-handed). Insert hook into next stitch to the right (left), under loop on hook, and draw up a loop. Yarn over and draw through all loops on hook.

NOTE
Three Squares are made, then crocheted together to make the Ruana.

SQUARES (make 3)
Wrap yarn around index finger. Insert hook into ring on finger, yarn over and draw up a loop. Carefully slip ring from finger and work the stitches of Row 1 into the ring.

Row 1: Ch 3 (counts as dc), (dc, ch 3, 2 dc) in ring – you will have 4 dc and a center ch-3 sp in this row. Gently but firmly, pull tail to tighten center of ring.

Row 2: Ch 3 (counts as dc), turn, dc in next dc, (2 dc, ch 3, 2 dc) in center ch-3 sp, dc in next dc, dc in top of beg ch-3 – 8 dc and a center ch-3 sp (4 dc on each side of center ch-3 sp).

Row 3: Ch 3 (counts as dc), turn, dc in next dc and each dc to center ch-3 sp, (2 dc, ch 3, 2 dc) in center ch-3 sp, dc in each dc to beg ch, dc in top of beg ch-3 – 12 dc and a center ch-3 sp (6 dc on each side of center ch-3 sp).

Rows 4 and 5: Rep Row 3 twice – 20 dc and a center ch-3 sp (10 dc on each side of center ch-3 sp) in Row 5.

Row 6: Ch 3 (counts as dc), turn, dc in next 9 dc, ch 1, (dc, ch 3, dc) in center ch-3 sp, ch 1, dc in next 9 dc, dc in top of beg ch-3 – (10 dc, ch 1, 1 dc) on each side of center ch-3 sp.

Row 7: Ch 3 (counts as dc), turn, dc in next 9 dc, ch 1, sk next ch-1 sp, dc in next dc, (2 dc, ch 3, 2 dc) in center ch-3 sp, dc in next dc, ch 1, sk next ch-1 sp, dc in next 9 dc, dc in top of beg ch-3 – (10 dc, ch 1, 3 dc) on each side of center ch-3 sp.

Row 8: Ch 3 (counts as dc), turn, dc in next 9 dc, ch 1, sk next ch-1 sp, dc in next 3 dc, (2 dc, ch 3, 2 dc) in center ch-3 sp, dc in next 3 dc, ch 1, sk next ch-1 sp, dc in next 9 dc, dc in top of beg ch-3 – (10 dc, ch 1, 5 dc) on each side of center ch-3 sp.

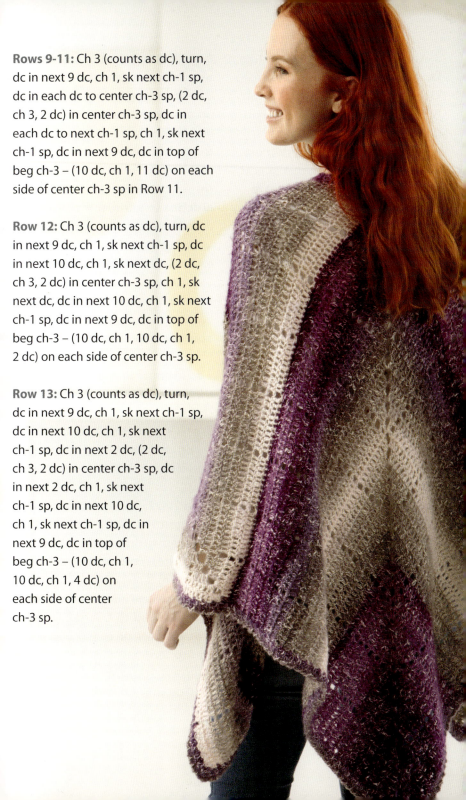

Rows 9-11: Ch 3 (counts as dc), turn, dc in next 9 dc, ch 1, sk next ch-1 sp, dc in each dc to center ch-3 sp, (2 dc, ch 3, 2 dc) in center ch-3 sp, dc in each dc to next ch-1 sp, ch 1, sk next ch-1 sp, dc in next 9 dc, dc in top of beg ch-3 – (10 dc, ch 1, 11 dc) on each side of center ch-3 sp in Row 11.

Row 12: Ch 3 (counts as dc), turn, dc in next 9 dc, ch 1, sk next ch-1 sp, dc in next 10 dc, ch 1, sk next dc, (2 dc, ch 3, 2 dc) in center ch-3 sp, ch 1, sk next dc, dc in next 10 dc, ch 1, sk next ch-1 sp, dc in next 9 dc, dc in top of beg ch-3 – (10 dc, ch 1, 10 dc, ch 1, 2 dc) on each side of center ch-3 sp.

Row 13: Ch 3 (counts as dc), turn, dc in next 9 dc, ch 1, sk next ch-1 sp, dc in next 10 dc, ch 1, sk next ch-1 sp, dc in next 2 dc, (2 dc, ch 3, 2 dc) in center ch-3 sp, dc in next 2 dc, ch 1, sk next ch-1 sp, dc in next 10 dc, ch 1, sk next ch-1 sp, dc in next 9 dc, dc in top of beg ch-3 – (10 dc, ch 1, 10 dc, ch 1, 4 dc) on each side of center ch-3 sp.

Rows 14-16: Ch 3 (counts as dc), turn, dc in next 9 dc, ch 1, sk next ch-1 sp, dc in next 10 dc, ch 1, sk next ch-1 sp, dc in each dc to center ch-3 sp, (2 dc, ch 3, 2 dc) in center ch-3 sp, dc in each dc to next ch-1 sp, ch 1, sk next ch-1 sp, dc in next 10 dc, ch 1, sk next ch-1 sp, dc in next 9 dc, dc in top of beg ch-3 – (10 dc, ch 1, 10 dc, ch 1, 10 dc) on each side of center ch-3 sp in Row 16.

Row 17: Ch 3 (counts as dc), turn, dc in next 9 dc, *ch 1, sk next ch-1 sp, dc in next 10 dc; rep from * once more, ch 1, (dc, ch 3, dc) in center ch-3 sp, ch 1, **dc in next 10 dc, ch 1, sk next ch-1 sp; rep from ** once more, dc in next 9 dc, dc in top of beg ch-3 – (10 dc, ch 1) 3 times and 1 dc on each side of center ch-3 sp.

Row 18: Ch 3 (counts as dc), turn, dc in next 9 dc, *ch 1, sk next ch-1 sp, dc in next 10 dc; rep from * once more, ch 1, sk next ch-1 sp, dc in next dc, (2 dc, ch 3, 2 dc) in center ch-3 sp, dc in next dc, ch 1, sk next ch-1 sp, **dc in next 10 dc, ch 1, sk next ch-1 sp; rep from ** once more, dc in next 9 dc, dc in top of beg ch-3 – (10 dc, ch 1) 3 times and 3 dc on each side of center ch-3 sp.

Rows 19-22: Ch 3 (counts as dc), turn, dc in next 9 dc, *ch 1, sk next ch-1 sp, dc in next 10 dc; rep from * once more, ch 1, sk next ch-1 sp, dc in each dc to center ch-3 sp, (2 dc, ch 3, 2 dc) in center ch-3 sp, dc in each dc to next ch-1 sp, ch 1, sk next ch-1 sp, **dc in next 10 dc, ch 1, sk next ch-1 sp; rep from ** once more, dc in next 9 dc, dc in top of beg ch-3 – (10 dc, ch 1) 3 times and 11 dc on each side of center ch-3 sp in Row 22.

Row 23: Ch 3 (counts as dc), turn, dc in next 9 dc, *ch 1, sk next ch-1 sp, dc in next 10 dc; rep from * 2 more times, ch 1, sk next dc, (2 dc, ch 3, 2 dc) in center ch-3 sp, ch 1, sk next dc, **dc in next 10 dc, ch 1, sk next ch-1 sp; rep from ** 2 more times, dc in next 9 dc, dc in top of beg ch-3 – (10 dc, ch 1) 4 times and 2 dc on each side of center ch-3 sp.

Rows 24-27: Ch 3 (counts as dc), turn, dc in next 9 dc, *ch 1, sk next ch-1 sp, dc in next 10 dc; rep from * 2 more times, ch 1, sk next ch-1 sp, dc in each dc to center ch-3 sp, (2 dc, ch 3, 2 dc) in center ch-3 sp, dc in each dc to next ch-1 sp, ch 1, sk next ch-1 sp, **dc in next 10 dc, ch 1, sk next ch-1 sp; rep from ** 2 more times, dc in next 9 dc, dc in top of beg ch-3 – (10 dc, ch 1) 4 times and 10 dc on each side of center ch-3 sp in Row 27.

Row 28: Ch 3 (counts as dc), turn, dc in next 9 dc, *ch 1, sk next ch-1 sp, dc in next 10 dc; rep from * 3 more times, ch 1, (dc, ch 3, dc) in center ch-3 sp, ch 1, **dc in next 10 dc, ch 1, sk next ch-1 sp; rep from ** 3 more times, dc in next 9 dc, dc in top of beg ch-3 – (10 dc, ch 1) 5 times and 1 dc on each side of center ch-3 sp.

Row 29: Ch 3 (counts as dc), turn, dc in next 9 dc, *ch 1, sk next ch-1 sp, dc in next 10 dc; rep from * 3 more times, ch 1, sk next ch-1 sp, dc in next dc, (2 dc, ch 3, 2 dc) in center ch-3 sp, dc in next dc, ch 1, sk next ch-1 sp, **dc in next 10 dc, ch 1, sk next ch-1 sp; rep from ** 3 more times, dc in next 9 dc, dc in top of beg ch-3 – (10 dc, ch 1) 5 times and 3 dc on each side of center ch-3 sp.

Rows 30-33: Ch 3 (counts as dc), turn, dc in next 9 dc, *ch 1, sk next ch-1 sp, dc in next 10 dc; rep from * 3 more times, ch 1, sk next ch-1 sp, dc in each dc to center ch-3 sp, (2 dc, ch 3, 2 dc) in center ch-3 sp, dc in each dc to next ch-1 sp, ch 1, sk next ch-1 sp, **dc in next 10 dc, ch 1, sk next ch-1 sp; rep from ** 3 more times, dc in next 9 dc, dc in top of beg ch-3 – (10 dc, ch 1) 5 times and 11 dc on each side of center ch-3 sp in Row 33.

Row 34: Ch 3 (counts as dc), turn, dc in next 9 dc, *ch 1, sk next ch-1 sp, dc in next 10 dc; rep from * 4 more times, ch 1, sk next dc, (2 dc, ch 3, 2 dc) in center ch-3 sp, ch 1, sk next dc, **dc in next 10 dc, ch 1, sk next ch-1 sp; rep from ** 4 more times, dc in next 9 dc, dc in top of beg ch-3 – (10 dc, ch 1) 6 times and 2 dc on each side of center ch-3 sp.

Rows 35-38: Ch 3 (counts as dc), turn, dc in next 9 dc, *ch 1, sk next ch-1 sp, dc in next 10 dc; rep from * 4 more times, ch 1, sk next ch-1 sp, dc in each dc to center ch-3 sp, (2 dc, ch 3, 2 dc) in center ch-3 sp, dc in each dc to next ch-1 sp, ch 1, sk next ch-1 sp, **dc in next 10 dc, ch 1, sk next ch-1 sp; rep from ** 4 more times, dc in next 9 dc, dc in top of beg ch-3 – (10 dc, ch 1) 6 times and 10 dc on each side of center ch-3 sp in Row 38.

Row 39: Ch 3 (counts as dc), turn, dc in next 9 dc, *ch 1, sk next ch-1 sp, dc in next 10 dc; rep from * 5 more times, ch 1, (dc, ch 3, dc) in center ch-3 sp, ch 1, **dc in next 10 dc, ch 1, sk next ch-1 sp; rep from ** 5 more times, dc in next 9 dc, dc in top of beg ch-3 – (10 dc, ch 1) 7 times and 1 dc on each side of center ch-3 sp.

Row 40: Ch 3 (counts as dc), turn, dc in next 9 dc, *ch 1, sk next ch-1 sp, dc in next 10 dc; rep from * 5 more times, ch 1, sk next ch-1 sp, dc in next dc, (2 dc, ch 3, 2 dc) in center ch-3 sp, dc in next dc, ch 1, sk next ch-1 sp, **dc in next 10 dc, ch 1, sk next ch-1 sp; rep from ** 5 more times, dc in next 9 dc, dc in top of beg ch-3 – (10 dc, ch 1) 7 times and 3 dc on each side of center ch-3 sp.

Rows 41-43: Ch 3 (counts as dc), turn, dc in next 9 dc, *ch 1, sk next ch-1 sp, dc in next 10 dc; rep from * 5 more times, ch 1, sk next ch-1 sp, dc in each dc to center ch-3 sp, (2 dc, ch 3, 2 dc) in center ch-3 sp, dc in each dc to next ch-1 sp, ch 1, sk next ch-1 sp, **dc in next 10 dc, ch 1, sk next ch-1 sp; rep from ** 5 more times, dc in next 9 dc, dc in top of beg ch-3 – (10 dc, ch 1) 7 times and 9 dc on each side of center ch-3 sp in Row 43. Fasten off.

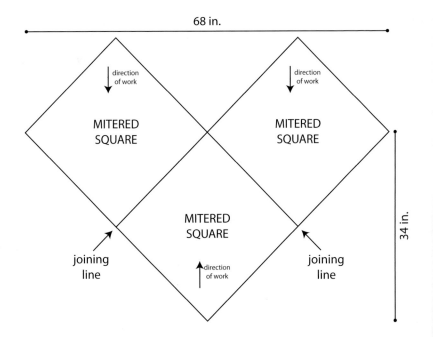

68 in.

direction of work

MITERED SQUARE

direction of work

MITERED SQUARE

MITERED SQUARE

34 in.

joining line

direction of work

joining line

FINISHING

Join Squares

Arrange Squares following Layout Diagram matching ch-1 sps along side edges of neighboring Squares. From WS, beg at outer edge of Ruana, join yarn at beg of side edges of two Squares to be joined by inserting hook in corner ch-3 sp of one Square and top of first dc of neighboring Square, yarn over and draw through all loops on hook (first sl st made), **working through both thicknesses, sl st in each dc to next ch-1 sp, *ch 1, sk next ch-1 sp, sl st in each dc to next ch-sp; rep from * all the way across side edge to join Squares and working last sl st in corner ch-3 sp ***, sl st in same corner ch-3 sp and top of dc of next neighboring Square to beg joining next side edges, rep from ** to ***.

Fasten off.

Border

Rnd 1 (RS): From RS, join yarn with a sc in end of joining line on right side edge of Ruana (join to left side edge if you crochet left handed), *ch 1, sk next dc or ch-1 sp, sc in next st; rep from * to next corner, ch 1, (sc, ch 1, sc) in corner; working in ends of rows, **ch 1, (sc, ch 1, sc) in end of next row; rep from ** to next corner, ch 1, (sc, ch 1, sc) in corner. Continue to work sc, ch 1 in this same way all the way around the outside edge, end with ch 1; join with sl st in first sc.

Rnd 2 (WS): Ch 1, turn, *sc in next ch-1 sp, ch 1, sk next sc; rep from * around, working (sc, ch 1, sc) in each corner ch-1 sp; join with sl st in first sc.

Rnd 3 (RS): Rep Rnd 2.

Rnd 4 (RS): Do not turn, *rev sc in next ch-1 sp, ch 1, sk next sc; rep from * around.

Fasten off.

Weave in ends.

Circle Shawlette

SIZE

Finished Diameter: About 27" (68.5 cm)

 **EASY +**

SHOPPING LIST

Yarn (Medium Weight) [4]

LION BRAND® SHAWL IN A BALL® (Art. #828)

- ☐ #200 Community Coral - 1 ball

Crochet Hook

LION BRAND® crochet hook

- ☐ Size I-9 (5.5 mm)
  - **or** size needed for gauge

Additional Supply

- ☐ LION BRAND® large-eyed blunt needle

GAUGE

Rnds 1-3 = about 4" (10 cm).

BE SURE TO CHECK YOUR GAUGE.

STITCH GUIDE

BEGINNING 2 DOUBLE CROCHET CLUSTER (abbreviated beg 2-dc Cl)
Ch 3, yarn over, insert hook in indicated st and draw up a loop, yarn over and draw through 2 loops on hook (2 loops rem on hook); yarn over and draw through rem 2 loops on hook.

2 DOUBLE CROCHET CLUSTER (abbreviated 2-dc Cl)
Yarn over, insert hook in indicated st and draw up a loop, yarn over and draw through 2 loops on hook (2 loops rem on hook), yarn over, insert hook in same st and draw up a loop, yarn over and draw through 2 loops on hook, yarn over and draw through all 3 loops on hook.

BEGINNING 3 DOUBLE CROCHET CLUSTER (abbreviated beg 3-dc Cl)
Ch 3, yarn over, insert hook in indicated st and draw up a loop, yarn over and draw through 2 loops on hook (2 loops rem on hook); yarn over, insert hook in same st and draw up a loop, yarn over and draw through 2 loops on hook, yarn over and draw through all 3 loops on hook.

3 DOUBLE CROCHET CLUSTER (abbreviated 3-dc Cl)
Yarn over, insert hook in indicated st, yarn over and draw up a loop, yarn over and draw through 2 loops on hook (2 loops rem on hook), (yarn over, insert hook in same st, yarn over and draw up a loop, yarn over and draw through 2 loops on hook) twice; yarn over and draw through all 4 loops on hook.

NOTE
Shawlette is worked in one piece in joined rnds with RS always facing. Do not turn at beg of rnds.

SHAWLETTE
Ch 6; join with sl st in first ch to form a ring.

Rnd 1 (RS): Ch 3 (counts as first dc), work 11 more dc in ring; join with sl st in top of beg ch – you will have 12 dc in this rnd.

Rnd 2: Sl st to next sp between sts, sc in same sp, *ch 1, sc in next sp between sts; rep from * around, ch 1; join with sl st in first sc – 12 sc and 12 ch-1 sps.

Rnd 3: Sl st to next ch-1 sp, beg 3-dc Cl in same ch-1 sp, *ch 2, 3-dc Cl in next ch-1 sp; rep from * around, ch 2; join with sl st in top of beg 3-dc Cl – 12 Cl and 12 ch-2 sps.

Rnd 4: Sl st to next ch-2 sp, (beg 2-dc Cl, ch 1, 2-dc Cl) in same ch-2 sp, *ch 1, (2-dc Cl, ch 1, 2-dc Cl) in next ch-2 sp; rep from * around, ch 1; join with sl st in top of beg 2-dc Cl – 24 Cl and 24 ch-1 sps.

Rnd 5: Sl st to next ch-1 sp, 2 sc in same ch-1 sp, *ch 1, 2 sc in next ch-1 sp; rep from * around, ch 1; join with sl st in first sc – 48 sc and 24 ch-1 sps.

Rnd 6: Sl st to next ch-1 sp, ch 3 (counts as dc), 2 dc in same ch-1 sp, 3 dc in each rem ch-1 sp around; join with sl st in top of beg ch – Twenty-four 3-dc groups.

Rnd 7: Sl to next st, sc in same st, *ch 1, sk next st, sc in next st; rep from * to last st, ch 1, sk last st; join with sl st in first sc – 36 sc and 36 ch-1 sps.

Rnd 8: (Sl st, beg 3-dc Cl) in first ch-1 sp, *ch 2, 3-dc Cl in next ch-1 sp; rep from * around, ch 2; join with sl st in top of beg 3-dc Cl – 36 Cl and 36 ch-2 sps.

Rnd 9: Sl st to next ch-2 sp, (beg 2-dc Cl, ch 1, 2-dc Cl) in same ch-2 sp, ch 1, 2-dc Cl in next ch-2 sp, *ch 1, (2-dc Cl, ch 1, 2-dc Cl) in next ch-2 sp, ch 1, 2-dc Cl in next ch-2 sp; rep from * around, ch 1; join with sl st in top of beg 2-dc Cl – 54 Cl and 54 ch-1 sps.

Rnd 14: Sl st to next ch-2 sp, (beg 2-dc Cl, ch 1, 2-dc Cl) in same ch-2 sp, (ch 1, 2-dc Cl in next ch-2 sp) twice, *ch 1, (2-dc Cl, ch 1, 2-dc Cl) in next ch-2 sp, (ch 1, 2-dc Cl in next ch-2 sp) twice; rep from * around, ch 1; join with sl st in top of beg 2-dc Cl – 72 Cl and 72 ch-1 sps.

Rnd 15: Rep Rnd 10 – 72 sc-groups.

Rnd 16: Rep Rnd 11 – 72 dc-groups.

Rnd 17: Rep Rnd 12 – 72 sc and 72 ch-1 sps.

Rnd 18: Rep Rnd 13 – 72 Cl and 72 ch-2 sps.

Rnd 19: Sl st to next ch-2 sp, (beg 2-dc Cl, ch 1, 2-dc Cl) in same ch-2 sp, (ch 1, 2-dc Cl in next ch-2 sp) 3 times, *ch 1, (2-dc Cl, ch 1, 2-dc Cl) in next ch-2 sp, (ch 1, 2-dc Cl in next ch-2 sp) 3 times; rep from * around, ch 1; join with sl st in top of beg 2-dc Cl – 90 Cl and 90 ch-1 sps.

Rnd 20: Rep Rnd 10 – 90 sc-groups.

Rnd 21: Rep Rnd 11 – 90 dc-groups.

Rnd 22: Rep Rnd 12 – 90 sc and 90 ch-1 sps.

Rnd 23: Rep Rnd 13 – 90 Cl and 90 ch-2 sps.

Rnd 10: Sl st to next ch-1 sp, 2 sc in same ch-1 sp, 2 sc in each rem ch-1 sp around; join with sl st in first sc – Fifty-four 2-sc groups.

Rnd 11: Sl st to next sp between 2-sc groups, ch 3 (counts as dc), dc in same sp, 2 dc in each rem sp between 2-sc groups; join with sl st in top of beg ch – Fifty-four 2-dc groups.

Rnd 12: Sl st to next st, sc in same st, *ch 1, sk next st, sc in next st; rep from * to last st, ch 1, sk last st; join with sl st in first sc – 54 sc and 54 ch-1 sps.

Rnd 13: Sl st to next ch-1 sp, beg 3-dc Cl in same ch-1 sp, *ch 2, 3-dc Cl in next ch-1 sp; rep from * around, ch 2; join with sl st in top of beg 3-dc Cl – 54 Cl and 54 ch-2 sps.

Rnd 24: Sl st to next ch-2 sp, (beg 2-dc Cl, ch 1, 2-dc Cl) in same ch-2 sp, (ch 1, 2-dc Cl in next ch-2 sp) 4 times, *ch 1, (2-dc Cl, ch 1, 2-dc Cl) in next ch-2 sp, (ch 1, 2-dc Cl in next ch-2 sp) 4 times; rep from * around, ch 1; join with sl st in top of beg 2-dc Cl – 108 Cl and 108 ch-1 sps.

Rnd 25: Rep Rnd 10 – 108 sc-groups.

Rnd 26: Rep Rnd 11 – 108 dc-groups.

Rnd 27: Rep Rnd 12 – 108 sc and 108 ch-1 sps.

Rnd 28: Rep Rnd 13 – 108 Cl and 108 ch-2 sps.

Rnd 29: Sl st to next ch-2 sp, (beg 2-dc Cl, ch 1, 2-dc Cl) in same ch-2 sp, (ch 1, 2-dc Cl in next ch-2 sp) 5 times, *ch 1, (2-dc Cl, ch 1, 2-dc Cl) in next ch-2 sp, (ch 1, 2-dc Cl in next ch-2 sp) 5 times; rep from * around, ch 1; join with sl st in top of beg 2-dc Cl – 126 Cl and 126 ch-1 sps.

Rnd 30: Rep Rnd 10 – 126 sc-groups.

Rnd 31: Rep Rnd 11 – 126 dc-groups.

Rnd 32: Rep Rnd 12 – 126 sc and 126 ch-1 sps.

Rnd 33: Rep Rnd 13 – 126 Cl and 126 ch-2 sps.

Rnd 34: Sl st to next ch-2 sp, (beg 2-dc Cl, ch 1, 2-dc Cl) in same ch-2 sp, (ch 1, 2-dc Cl in next ch-2 sp) 6 times, *ch 1, (2-dc Cl, ch 1, 2-dc Cl) in next ch-2 sp, (ch 1, 2-dc Cl in next ch-2 sp) 6 times; rep from * around, ch 1; join with sl st in top of beg 2-dc Cl – 144 Cl and 144 ch-1 sps.

Rnd 35: Rep Rnd 10 – 144 sc-groups.

Rnd 36: Rep Rnd 11 – 144 dc-groups.

Rnd 37: Ch 1, sc in each st around – 288 sc.
Fasten off.

FINISHING
Weave in ends.

Triangular Shawl

SIZE

About 47½" x 25" (120.5 cm x 63.5 cm)

SHOPPING LIST

Yarn (Medium Weight) 🪢4

LION BRAND® SHAWL IN A BALL® (Art. #828)

☐   #201 Restful Rainbow - 1 ball

Crochet Hook

LION BRAND® crochet hook

☐   Size J-10 (6 mm) **or** size needed for gauge

Additional Supply

☐   LION BRAND® large-eyed blunt needle

GAUGE

8 (dc, ch 1) groups = about 4" (10 cm).

BE SURE TO CHECK YOUR GAUGE.

STITCH GUIDE

2 DOUBLE CROCHET CLUSTER
(abbreviated Cl)

Yarn over, insert hook in indicated st and draw up a loop, yarn over and draw through 2 loops on hook (2 loops rem on hook), yarn over, insert hook in same st and draw up a loop, yarn over and draw through 2 loops on hook, yarn over and draw through all 3 loops on hook.

CLUSTER V-STITCH
(abbreviated Cl-V)

Work (Cl, ch 1, Cl) in indicated st or sp.

CENTER CLUSTER V-STITCH
(abbreviated Center Cl-V)

Work (Cl, ch 3, Cl) in indicated st or sp.

NOTES

1. Shawl is worked in one piece, back and forth in rows, in an easy pattern, beginning at center back neck.
2. For those who find a visual helpful, we have provided a stitch diagram.

SHAWL

Ch 6.

Row 1: (Tr, ch 3, tr, ch 1, tr) in 6th ch from hook (5 skipped ch count as tr, ch 1) – you will have 4 tr, 2 ch-1 sps, and a center ch-3 sp in this row.

Row 2: Ch 4 (counts as dc, ch 1 in this row and in all following rows), turn, sk first ch-1 sp, Cl-V in next st, ch 1, Center Cl-V in center ch-3 sp, ch 1, Cl-V in next st, ch 1, dc in 5th ch of beg ch – 1 Center Cl-V, 2 Cl-V, 4 ch-1 sps and a dc at beg and end of this row.

Row 3: Ch 4, turn, sk first ch-1 sp, Cl-V in ch-1 sp of first Cl-V, ch 1, dc in next ch-1 sp, ch 1, Center Cl-V in center ch-3 sp, ch 1, dc in next ch-1 sp, ch 1, Cl-V in ch-1 sp of next Cl-V, ch 1, dc in 3rd ch of beg ch-4 – 1 Center Cl-V, 2 Cl-V, 6 ch-1 sps, and 4 dc.

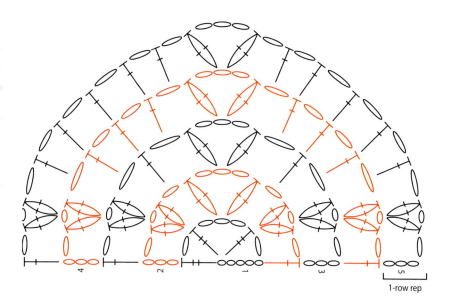

Row 4: Ch 4, turn, sk first ch-1 sp, Cl-V in ch-1 sp of first Cl-V, ch 1, dc in next ch-1 sp, ch 1, dc in next dc, ch 1, dc in next ch-1 sp, ch 1, Center Cl-V in center ch-3 sp, ch 1, dc in next ch-1 sp, ch 1, dc in next dc, ch 1, dc in next ch-1 sp, ch 1, Cl-V in ch-1 sp of next Cl-V, ch 1, dc in 3rd ch of beg ch-4 – 1 Center Cl-V, 2 Cl-V, 10 ch-1 sps, and 8 dc.

KEY

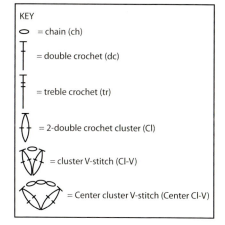

◯ = chain (ch)

= double crochet (dc)

= treble crochet (tr)

= 2-double crochet cluster (Cl)

= cluster V-stitch (Cl-V)

= Center cluster V-stitch (Center Cl-V)

Row 5: Ch 4, turn, sk first ch-1 sp, Cl-V in ch-1 sp of first Cl-V, ch 1, dc in next ch-1 sp, (ch 1, dc in next dc) to ch-1 sp before Center Cl-V, ch 1, dc in next ch-1 sp, ch 1, Center Cl-V in center ch-3 sp, ch 1, dc in next ch-1 sp, (ch 1, dc in next dc) to ch-1 sp before next Cl-V, ch 1, dc in next ch-1 sp, ch 1, Cl-V in ch-1 sp of next Cl-V, ch 1, dc in 3rd ch of beg ch-4 – 1 Center Cl-V, 2 Cl-V, 14 ch-1 sps, and 12 dc.

Rows 6-39: Repeat Row 5 for 34 more times – 1 Center Cl-V, 2 Cl-V, 150 ch-1 sps, and 148 dc. At the end of Row 39, do NOT fasten off.

Edging
Ch 1, do not turn, work sc evenly spaced around outside edge of Shawl.
Fasten off.

FINISHING
Weave in ends.

General Instructions

ABBREVIATIONS

beg = begin(ning)(s)
ch = chain
ch-sp(s) = chain space(s)
   previously made
cm = centimeters
dc = double crochet
hdc = half double crochet
mm = millimeters
rem = remain(ing)(s)
rep(s) = repeat(s)
RS = right side
rnd(s) = round(s)
sc = single crochet
sk = skip
sl st = slip stitch
sp(s) = space(s)
st(s) = stitch(es)
tog = together
WS = wrong side

* — When you see an asterisk used within a pattern row, the symbol indicates that later you will be told to repeat a portion of the instruction. Most often the instructions will say, repeat from * so many times.

( ) or [ ] — Sets off a short number of stitches that are repeated or indicates additional information.

– When you see – (dash) followed by a number of stitches, this tells you how many stitches you will have at the end of a row or round.

GAUGE

Never underestimate the importance of gauge. Achieving the correct gauge assures that the finished size of your piece matches the finished size given in the pattern.

CHECKING YOUR GAUGE

Work a swatch that is at least 4" (10 cm) square. Use the suggested hook size and the number of stitches given. If your swatch is larger than 4" (10 cm), you need to work it again using a smaller hook; if it is smaller than 4" (10 cm), try it with a larger hook. This might require a swatch or two to get the exact gauge given in the pattern.

METRICS

As a handy reference, keep in mind that 1 ounce = approximately 28 grams and 1" = 2.5 centimeters.

TERMS

fasten off — To end your piece, you need to simply cut and pull the yarn through the last loop left on the hook. This keeps the last stitch intact and prevents the work from unraveling.

right side — Refers to the front of the piece.

CROCHET HOOKS	
U.S.	Metric mm
B-1	2.25
C-2	2.75
D-3	3.25
E-4	3.5
F-5	3.75
G-6	4
7	4.5
H-8	5
I-9	5.5
J-10	6
K-10½	6.5
L-11	8
M/N-13	9
N/P-15	10
P/Q	15
Q	16
S	19

CROCHET TERMINOLOGY

UNITED STATES		INTERNATIONAL
slip stitch (slip st)	=	single crochet (sc)
single crochet (sc)	=	double crochet (dc)
half double crochet (hdc)	=	half treble crochet (htr)
double crochet (dc)	=	treble crochet (tr)
treble crochet (tr)	=	double treble crochet (dtr)
double treble crochet (dtr)	=	triple treble crochet (ttr)
triple treble crochet (tr tr)	=	quadruple treble crochet (qtr)
skip	=	miss

■□□□ **BEGINNER**	Projects for first-time crocheters using basic stitches. Minimal shaping.
■■□□ **EASY**	Projects using yarn with basic stitches, repetitive stitch patterns, simple color changes, and simple shaping and finishing.
■■■□ **INTERMEDIATE**	Projects using a variety of techniques, such as basic lace patterns or color patterns, mid-level shaping and finishing.
■■■■ **EXPERIENCED**	Projects with intricate stitch patterns, techniques and dimension, such as non-repeating patterns, multi-color techniques, fine threads, small hooks, detailed shaping and refined finishing.

Yarn Weight Symbol & Names	LACE 0	SUPER FINE 1	FINE 2	LIGHT 3	MEDIUM 4	BULKY 5	SUPER BULKY 6	JUMBO 7
Type of Yarns in Category	Fingering, size 10 crochet thread	Sock, Fingering, Baby	Sport, Baby	DK, Light Worsted	Worsted, Afghan, Aran	Chunky, Craft, Rug	Super Bulky, Roving	Jumbo, Roving
Crochet Gauge* Ranges in Single Crochet to 4" (10 cm)	32-42 sts**	21-32 sts	16-20 sts	12-17 sts	11-14 sts	8-11 sts	6-9 sts	5 sts and fewer
Advised Hook Size Range	Steel*** 6 to 8, Regular hook B-1	B-1 to E-4	E-4 to 7	7 to I-9	I-9 to K-10½	K-10½ to M/N-13	M/N-13 to Q	Q and larger

*GUIDELINES ONLY: The chart above reflects the most commonly used gauges and hook sizes for specific yarn categories.

** Lace weight yarns are usually crocheted with larger hooks to create lacy openwork patterns. Accordingly, a gauge range is difficult to determine. Always follow the gauge stated in your pattern.

*** Steel crochet hooks are sized differently from regular hooks–the higher the number, the smaller the hook, which is the reverse of regular hook sizing.

LION BRAND® SHAWL IN A BALL®

Article #828

Weight Category: 4 - Medium Weight: Fashion and accessories

Stripes & Metallic: 5.3oz/150g (518yd/473m)
Stripes: - 58% Cotton, 39% Acrylic, 3% other
Metallic: - 61% Cotton, 34% Acrylic, 5% other

Gauge:

Knit: 20 sts x 28 rows = 4 inches on size 6 [4 mm] needles
Crochet: 14 sc x 19 rows = 4 inches on G-6 [4 mm] hook

Product Care Instructions: Handwash and lay flat to dry.

VISIT LionBrand.com FOR:

• Learn to Knit & Crochet Instructions
• Weekly newsletter with articles, tips, and updates

• Store Locator